WATCHING THE SKY IN NATURE

BY ABBY COLICH

BLUE OWL
BOOKS

TIPS FOR CAREGIVERS

Social and emotional learning (SEL) helps children manage emotions, learn how to feel empathy, create and achieve goals, and make good decisions. One goal of teaching SEL skills is to help children care for themselves, others, and the world around them. The more time children spend in nature and the more they learn about it, the more likely they will be to appreciate it and receive its emotional benefits.

BEFORE READING

Talk to the reader about spending time in nature. Ask what he or she knows about the sky.

Discuss: Do you spend time outside? Do you feel different when you are outdoors instead of indoors? What are some things you can watch in the sky?

AFTER READING

Talk to the reader about how looking at the sky makes him or her feel.

Discuss: Think of a time you've had negative feelings or when your body felt tense or tired. How could being in nature and looking at the sky make you feel better?

SEL GOAL

Children may struggle with processing their emotions, and they may lack accessible tools to help them do so. Explain to children that nature can help people feel good. Nature is always available to them, even if they are just looking out the window or looking at pictures of natural scenes. Encourage children to focus on the sky the next time they are struggling with their emotions. Ask them to observe how it makes them feel.

TABLE OF CONTENTS

CHAPTER 1

WHY WATCH THE SKY?

Look outside. Then look up! The sky is full of sights to **observe**. What do you see?

Do you see clouds in the sky? Maybe you can make out shapes in them. Or maybe a storm is rolling in. On clear nights, you might see stars.

Do you ever feel **tense**, angry, or afraid? Watching the sky can help you feel less **stressed**. When we **focus** on what's happening in nature, we are practicing **mindfulness**. We are being **present** in the world around us.

GOOD FOR YOUR BODY

As you practice mindfulness, your mind and body will feel better. You may feel less tense. You may have more **energy** or sleep better at night.

CHAPTER 2

HOW TO WATCH THE SKY

Watching the sky is easy. It is always there. Just be sure to dress for the weather before heading outdoors. If it is sunny, have a pair of sunglasses handy. Always make sure you are in a safe place with a trusted adult or that you have an adult's permission to be outside.

Since you may be sitting still, you will want to be comfortable. You can bring a towel or blanket to sit on. Look up at the sky. What do you see?

Think about your other senses, too.
Paying attention to your senses
can help you be more focused.
Do you feel the sun's warmth
on your skin? Do you feel or
hear the wind blowing?
Do you smell flowers?

CHAPTER 3

WAYS TO WATCH THE SKY

You can watch the sky any time of day. In the early morning, watch the sun rise. Try to **appreciate** all the colors. Take this time to wake up your mind. What will you do today? Tell yourself you can handle whatever comes your way.

In the evening, watch the sun set. Is something bothering you? Picture it sinking away like the setting sun. How do you feel?

You can watch weather, too. Think about clouds slowly moving away after a storm. Now picture **anxious** feelings or bad moods leaving your mind in the same way. Is it easier to focus?

LOOK FOR A RAINBOW

When the sun comes out after the rain, look for a rainbow! Look in the opposite direction of the sun. A rainbow often only lasts a few minutes. Take time to **admire** it. When you focus on an event while it's happening, you might enjoy it more.

At night, you can **stargaze**. Look for stars and planets. Do the stars make shapes? These are **constellations**. Try to make your mind and body still like the stars. Being still can help you sleep better.

Look at the moon each night. Do you notice how its shape seems to change? These are called **phases**. Each month, the phases start over. Have you had a bad day? Remember that you can always start over and try to make something better.

If you can't go outside, look out a window. Or look at photos of the sky. You can also close your eyes and imagine it. What does it look like? How does it make you feel?

Look at the sky at least once a day. Make it a **routine**. Use this time to slow your mind and refocus.

When you look at the sky, appreciate what is there. You might start to appreciate more things in your life. When you feel **grateful**, you feel better about yourself.

DIFFERENT TIMES

Try watching the sky at different times of the day. See what works best for you. The sky has something new to offer every time of the day!

GOALS AND TOOLS

GROW WITH GOALS

Practice different ways of watching the sky. What helps you focus? What helps you calm down?

Goal: Try to look at the sky for a few minutes every day. Write down or draw a picture of what you see. Record the weather and time of day.

Goal: What is your favorite thing to see in the sky? Research or study the science behind it.

Goal: Try to recognize when you are getting upset. Remember that feelings come and go like clouds in the sky. Your mad and sad feelings won't last forever!

MINDFULNESS EXERCISE

Go to a quiet place outside. If you can't go outside, sit indoors near a window so you can see the sky or find a picture of the sky to look at. Sit up straight. Find an object to focus on. Continue to gaze at it for a few moments. Slowly breathe in and out. Think about the following questions.

1. How does your body feel?

2. What emotions do you feel?

3. Do you feel differently after this exercise?

GLOSSARY

admire
To think highly of.

anxious
Causing worry or nervousness.

appreciate
To enjoy or value somebody
or something.

constellations
Groups of stars that form
shapes in the sky.

energy
The ability or strength to do
things without getting tired.

focus
To concentrate on something.

grateful
Feeling or showing thanks.

mindfulness
A mentality achieved by focusing
on the present moment and calmly
recognizing and accepting your
feelings, thoughts, and sensations.

observe
To watch someone or something
closely, especially to learn something.

phases
Ways that the moon looks
in its series of changes.

present
Being in one place
and not elsewhere.

routine
A practiced sequence of actions.

stargaze
To look at stars.

stressed
Experiencing mental
or emotional strain.

tense
Stretched stiff and tight,
or unable to relax.

TO LEARN MORE

FACT SURFER

Finding more information is as easy as 1, 2, 3.

1. Go to www.factsurfer.com

2. Enter "**watchingtheskyinnature**" into the search box.

3. Choose your book to see a list of websites.

INDEX

Blue Owl Books are published by Jump!, 5357 Penn Avenue South, Minneapolis, MN 55419, www.jumplibrary.com

Copyright © 2021 Jump! International copyright reserved in all countries. No part of this book may be reproduced in any form without written permission from the publisher.

Library of Congress Cataloging-in-Publication Data

Names: Colich, Abby, author.
Title: Watching the sky in nature / by Abby Colich.
Description: Minneapolis, MN: Jump!, Inc., [2021]
Series: Nature heals | Includes index. | Audience: Ages 7–10
Identifiers: LCCN 2020028987 (print)
LCCN 2020028988 (ebook)
ISBN 9781645278498 (hardcover)
ISBN 9781645278504 (paperback)
ISBN 9781645278511 (ebook)
Subjects: LCSH: Nature—Psychological aspects—Juvenile literature. | Sky—Juvenile literature.
Nature, Healing power of—Juvenile literature. | Mind and body—Juvenile literature.
Classification: LCC BF353.5.N37 C65 2021 (print) | LCC BF353.5.N37 (ebook) | DDC 155.4/18915—dc23
LC record available at https://lccn.loc.gov/2020028987
LC ebook record available at https://lccn.loc.gov/2020028988

Editor: Eliza Leahy
Designer: Michelle Sonnek

Photo Credits: bubutu/Shutterstock, cover; Roman Kondrashov/Shutterstock, 1; photobeps/Shutterstock, 3; drbimages/iStock, 4; irin-k/Shutterstock, 5; nojustice/iStock, 6–7; Ronnachai Palas/Shutterstock, 8; Studio Romantic/Shutterstock, 9; belushi/Shutterstock, 10–11; mrfiza/Shutterstock, 12; Iryna Mylinska/iStock, 13; Beauty photographer/Shutterstock, 14–15; Andrey_Rut/Shutterstock, 16–17; PeopleImages/iStock, 18–19; Maltsev Ilya/Shutterstock, 20–21.

Printed in the United States of America at Corporate Graphics in North Mankato, Minnesota.